NEW YORK REVIEW BOOKS
CLASSICS

GENERATIONS

LUCILLE CLIFTON (1936–2010) was an American poet
known for her work celebrating the African American female
experience and family life. She is best known for her collections
Good Times, *Two-Headed Woman*, *Next*, *Good Woman*, *Blessing
the Boats* (winner of the National Book Award), and *Quilting*.
The only author to have two books of poetry nominated for a
Pulitzer Prize in the same year, she was awarded the Ruth Lilly
Poetry Prize and the Robert Frost Medal for Lifetime Achieve-
ment from the Poetry Society of America. In addition to her
poetry collections, Clifton also wrote numerous books for
children, including her Everett Anderson series. Her literary
legacy is being carried forward with the Clifton House, a writer
and artist workshop space based in her beloved former home in
Baltimore.

TRACY K. SMITH is a writer and former United States
Poet Laureate. The author of a memoir, *Ordinary Light*, and
four poetry collections, including *Life on Mars*, which won
the Pulitzer Prize in 2012, she currently serves as the chair of
Princeton University's Lewis Center for the Arts.

GENERATIONS

A Memoir

LUCILLE CLIFTON

NEW YORK REVIEW BOOKS

New York

THIS IS A NEW YORK REVIEW BOOK
PUBLISHED BY THE NEW YORK REVIEW OF BOOKS
435 Hudson Street, New York, NY 10014
www.nyrb.com

First published as a New York Review Books Classic in 2021.

Library of Congress Cataloging-in-Publication Data
Names: Clifton, Lucille, 1936–2010, author.
Title: Generations: a memoir / by Lucille Clifton.
Description: New York: New York Review Books, [2021] | Series: New York
  Review Books
Identifiers: LCCN 2020058364 (print) | LCCN 2020058365 (ebook) |
  ISBN 9781681375878 (paperback) | ISBN 9781681375885 (ebook)
Subjects: LCSH: Clifton, Lucille, 1936–2010. | African American poets—
  Biography. | Poets, American—20th century—Biography.
Classification: LCC PS3553.L45 Z46 2021 (print) | LCC PS3553.L45 (ebook) |
  DDC 811/.54—dc23
LC record available at https://lccn.loc.gov/2020058364
LC ebook record available at https://lccn.loc.gov/2020058365

ISBN 978-1-68137-587-8
Available as an electronic book; ISBN 978-1-68137-588-5

Printed in the United States of America on acid-free paper.
10 9 8 7 6 5 4 3 2 1

CONTENTS

INTRODUCTION

WHAT IS our relationship to history? Do we belong to it, or is it ours? Are we in it? Does it run through us, spilling out like water, or blood?

I think the answers to those questions, at least in America, depend upon who you are—or rather, on who you've been taught to believe that you are. If the history you descend from has been mapped, adapted, mythologized, reenacted, and broadcast as though it is the central defining story of a continent, perhaps you can be forgiven (up to a point) for having succumbed to a collective distortion.

But what if yours is a history the wider world once recorded not as lives and feats but as articles of inventory? Men, women, children listed according to their age and value as property? What if the largeness of those lives—what they endured, yes, but also what they carried, remembered, witnessed, and made—has been hushed up, negated, overwritten, or outright erased? What if the recovery of your full story sheds stark light on the lie of that other, louder story?

There it is: light. It took three paragraphs to creep in as a metaphor, though it runs through the work of Lucille Clifton like life force. Light comes to her. Light speaks. Light emanates from the figures of history and myth, like Lucifer—God's *bringer of light*—whom Clifton claims as her namesake, and who in her rendering testifies:

> illuminate i could
> and so
> illuminate i did

If light is what the work of Clifton is intent upon spreading, then I'm tempted to think that history as we have been conditioned to accept it is unrefracted, all of a piece, and blindingly white. Whereas Clifton's imagination is prismatic; it slows down the central story so we can see what it is truly made of: all the dazzling colors moving at different frequencies and, depending upon circumstances, in distinct directions.

In *Generations*, her poetically terse and emotionally epic prose memoir first published in 1976, Clifton uses the occasion of her father's funeral to attest to the lives lived and the marks made by the generations of people she descends from. First they are names, dates, and places. Like Caroline Donald—Mammy Ca'line—"born free among the Dahomey people in 1822 and died free in Bedford Virginia in 1910." To reinscribe these lives into recollected history is to restore history itself to a rightful state of commotion.

Once named, these kin arrive not singly but en masse, brought to life through the rhythm and inflection of voices—like the voice of Clifton's own father, Sam Sayles, in whose vernacular rhythm Mammy Ca'line is not merely described but rather conjured:

Oh she was tall and skinny and walked straight as a soldier, Lue. Straight like somebody marching wherever she went. And she talked with a Oxford accent! I ain't kidding. Don't let nobody tell you them old people was dumb. She talked like she was from London Eng-

land and when we kids would be running and hooping
and hollering all around she would come to the door
and look straight at me and shake her finger and say
"Stop that Bedlam, mister, stop that Bedlam, I say."
With a Oxford accent, Lue! She was a dark old skinny
lady and she raised my Daddy and then raised me, least
till I was eight years old when she died.

I hear, in Sayles's *Oh*s and his *Lue*s and his exclamations and
his insistence, something that is not simply expressive but
exultant and—positively—oracular. He is engaged not simply in an act of telling but of creating and consecrating a
capacity for belief and understanding in both his daughter
and—if we are listening properly—his daughter's readers.
The passage above segues seamlessly into the following
capacity-expanding moment, where Clifton's father signifies
upon how, at eight years of age, Mammy Ca'line "walked
North from New Orleans to Virginia in 1830," at which
point she was sold away from her family:

I remember everything she ever told me, cause you
know when you that age you old enough to remember
things. I remember everything she told me, Lue, even
though she died when I was eight years old. And then
I knowed about what she remembered cause that's how
old she was when she got here. Eight years old.

Mammy Ca'line's depth of feeling, knowledge, and loss—in
other words, the reality of her personhood—both affirmed
and was affirmed by the reality of young Sam Sayles's self-
hood. As a child in grief, he found depth of feeling and
knowledge, or generated it, through belief in what Mammy

Ca'line, in her own grief, would have been required to find or generate.

These are the lives that America's dominant history, as defined by aspirational notions of white personhood, has let fall into shadow. These are the stories that have been left unmarked and untended by America's preferred view of itself, like the graves of slaves on land passed down through the white generations. One of the major contributions of Clifton's writing is that she has teased out these lives, allowing them to demand their rightful space, to command our full attention, to teach us things about themselves and ourselves.

But it is not enough only to tease out, to separate and disband. Clifton's purpose is to teach us to see that we are, in fact, moving together and that we are, in fact, part of a large whole. If that whole is unified, unity is not what we have been taught to believe; it is not compliance, not assimilation, not an enforced hierarchy. Neither is it simply escape. What, then, is the vision of America that Clifton is intent upon illuminating?

When you arrange one prism next to another, all those different colors—red, orange, yellow, and so on—rejoin one another, and together they begin to move in another direction.

There is one more thing I want to ask you to consider, as you lose and perhaps find yourself in the generations of Clifton's family. I take as significant the fact that Walt Whitman's voice is invoked alongside the everyday poetry taken from the mouths of Clifton's ancestors. In this context, Whitman's "Song of Myself" is no longer a familiar American music but an invitation to a radical reconfiguring of self. In other words, when Whitman's "I celebrate myself, and sing myself, / And what I assume you shall assume, / For every atom belonging to me as good belongs to you" is sat beneath a portrait of Clifton's grandfather and great-grandmother, what I am made to understand is this: here in America, and perhaps everywhere, no matter who we have been made to believe that we are, we are—all of us—the children of slaves.

—TRACY K. SMITH
June 5, 2021

GENERATIONS

for
Samuel Louis Sayles, Sr.
Daddy
1902–1969
who is Somewhere,
being a Man

Lo, mine eye hath seen all this, mine ear hath heard and understood it.

What ye know, the same do I know also; I am not inferior unto you.

Job 13:1 and 2

Get what you want, you from Dahomey women.

—The woman called Caroline Donald Sale
born free in Afrika in 1822
died free in America in 1910

CAROLINE AND SON

I celebrate myself, and sing myself,
And what I assume you shall assume,
For every atom belonging to me as good belongs to you.

—WALT WHITMAN, "Song of Myself"

I

SHE SAID

I saw your notice in the Bedford newspaper and I thought isn't this interesting, so I figured I would call you and tell you that I am a Sale and I have compiled and privately printed a history of the Sale/Sayle family of Bedford County Virginia and I would be glad to send it to you. But why are you interested in the Sayles?

Her voice is sweet and white over the wires. What shall I say to this white lady? What does it matter now that Daddy is dead and I am a Clifton?

Have you ever heard of a man named John F. Sale? I ask.

Why yes, he was a great-uncle of mine, I believe. She is happy and excited.

Well, my maiden name was Sayles, I say.

What was your father's name? she asks. She is jumping through the wires.

Samuel, I say.

She is puzzled. I don't remember that name, she says.

*

Who remembers the names of the slaves? Only the children of slaves. The names are Caroline and Lucy and Samuel, I say. Slave names.

Ooooh, she cries. Oh that's just awful. And there is silence.

Then she tells me that the slave cabins are still there at the Sale home where she lives, and the graves of the slaves are there, unmarked. The graves of my family. She remembers the name Caroline, she says, her parents were delivered by the midwife, Mammy Caroline. The midwife Mammy Caroline.

Is the Nichols house still there? I ask.

Still with the family in it, she says. I hear the trouble in her voice.

And I rush to reassure her. Why? Is it in my blood to reassure this thin-voiced white lady? I am a Clifton now, I say. I only wanted to find out about these things. I am only curious, I say. It's a long time after, and I just wanted to know.

I can help you, she sighs. I can help you.

But I never hear her voice again.

Yet she sends the history she has compiled and in it are her family's names. And our family names are thick in her family like an omen. I see that she is the last of her line. Old and not married, left with a house and a name. I look at my husband and our six children and I feel the Dahomey women gathering in my bones.

"They called her Ca'line," Daddy would tell us. "What her African name was, I never heard her say. I asked her one time to tell me and she just shook her head. But it'll be forgot, I hollered at her, it'll be forgot. She just smiled at me and said 'Don't you worry, mister, don't you worry.'"

2

SHE SAID

he finished his eggs and his bacon and his coffee and said Jo get me one of them True Greens and I got him his cigarette and went upstairs to get a ashtray and when I got back he was laying on the floor and blood was all on his mouth like when Mama used to have her fits and I hollered Daddy Daddy Daddy and Bobby come running down the stairs to see what was the matter and when he saw he called the rescue squad but when they got here they said he was dead. I didn't believe it.

Punkin calling from Buffalo, talking soft and slow like she did when she was high. Lue, Lue, Daddy is dead.

I didn't believe her. I hung up the phone and went back to reading the paper and waited for Fred and Sammy to come back home. I didn't believe Mr. Sayles Lord was dead. I didn't believe Old Brother Sayles was dead. I didn't believe the Rock was dead. I didn't believe you were dead Daddy. You said you stayed on here because we had feet of clay. I didn't believe you could die Daddy. I didn't believe you would. I didn't want you to die Daddy. You always said you would haunt us if you did.

*

We drove North, seeing everything and laughing the whole way. Miss Mattie came and got the kids and I stopped by Sears and bought a black hat and Fred and Sammy got a map and we headed North, Fred driving.

Mammy Ca'line walked North from New Orleans to Virginia in 1830. She was eight years old.

3

"Mammy Ca'line raised me," Daddy would say. "After my Grandma Lucy died, she took care of Genie and then took care of me. She was my great-grandmother, Lucy's Mama, you know, but everybody called her Mammy like they did in them days. Oh she was tall and skinny and walked straight as a soldier, Lue. Straight like somebody marching wherever she went. And she talked with a Oxford accent! I ain't kidding. Don't let nobody tell you them old people was dumb. She talked like she was from London England and when we kids would be running and hooping and hollering all around she would come to the door and look straight at me and shake her finger and say 'Stop that Bedlam, mister, stop that Bedlam, I say.' With a Oxford accent, Lue! She was a dark old skinny lady and she raised my Daddy and then raised me, least till I was eight years old when she died. When I was eight years old. I remember everything she ever told me, cause you know when you that age you old enough to remember things. I remember everything she told me, Lue, even though she died when I was eight years old. And then I knowed about what she remembered cause that's how old she was when she got here. Eight years old."

4

Driving out of Baltimore you turn around narrow one-way streets and long-named alleys and stop in lines of school-teachers on Monday mornings. Every car had a woman driver except ours.

Where are the men, I laughed. On the corners, Sammy laughed back. Everything was funny. Everything was funny. We curved and crawled around past Ward's, past the last hamburger before the highway and broke out of the city like out of chains. Fred gunned the motor and laughed and we left Baltimore behind us. An old Black lady watched us making noise outside her country door. I could hear her head shaking. This is Maryland farm country, we be nice niggers here. I laughed at her frown. Fred nodded his head toward the front of the car. Be careful, he said, Pennsylvania is out there. We all laughed. Everything was funny.

"Walking from New Orleans to Virginia," Daddy would say, "you go through Mississippi, Alabama, Georgia, South Carolina and North Carolina. And that's the walk Mammy Ca'line took when she was eight years old. She was born among the Dahomey people in 1822, Lue. Among the Dahomey people, and she used to always say 'Get what you want, you from Dahomey women.' And she used to tell us

17

about how they had a whole army of nothing but women back there and how they was the best soldiers in the world. And she was from among the Dahomey people and one day her and her Mama and her sister and her brother was captured and throwed on a boat and on a boat till they landed in New Orleans. And I would ask her how did you get captured, Mammy, and she would say that she was a child and I would ask her when did it happen, Mammy, and she would say 'In 1830 I walked from New Orleans to Virginia and I was eight years old.' And I would ask her what was it like on the boat and she would just shake her head. And it seems like so long ago, you know, because when I was asking her this it must have been 1908 or '9. I was just a little boy. I was a little boy and my Mama was working in the tobacco plant and my Mammy Ca'line took care of me and I took care of my brothers and my sister. My Daddy Genie was dead. He died young. He was my real Grandmother Lucy's boy and of course she was dead too. Her name was Lucille just like my sister and just like you. You named for Dahomey women, Lue."

5

Pennsylvania seemed greener than Maryland did. It smelled like spring and even when we laughed at the Welcome to Pennsylvania sign we sniffed deeply the green spring smell. My brother said the only thing wrong with Pennsylvania was that it was full of Pennsylvanians and Fred grinned and then glanced into the rear-view mirror. Sammy and I looked behind us. There was a Pennsylvanian driving behind us, driving too close to our station wagon. A whiteboy driver in a cowboy hat driving a cowboy car and bent down low and stiff over the steering wheel. Sammy and I pointed at him and laughed loud and fell down all in the seat and the poor Pennsylvania whiteboy sat straight up and gunned around us three crazy spooks driving North and sped the hell in front of us and across the mountains scared and driving like hell. Like away from hell. Fred started to speed and we strained trying to catch up with him and laugh at him some more but we looked across every mountain and he was gone. We kept on, saying we were looking for our cowboy and followed the day across the Pennsylvania green until we left spring there in the high ground and the land turned slowly grey and hard and cracking and we were nearing New York State. The promised land.

6

"WHEN Mammy Ca'line and them got to Virginia," my Daddy would say, "the coffle was split up and she was sold to a man named Bob Donald. Her brother was sold to somebody in a close-by town and he was trained to be a blacksmith and her sister was sold to a plantation next to Bob Donald's and Mammy Ca'line got to see her sometime. Of course she never saw her Mama again cause she was sold away. Mammy Ca'line was eight years old. And I used to ask her, Mammy, don't you wish you could have seen your Mama sometime? And she would just shake her head. She never would say nothing to me about her Mama but sometime when I was a boy I would sit with her and Aunt Margaret Brown, who was her sister, while they rocked on the porch and I would hear them talking about do you remember different things. And they would say about Do you remember Nat Turner's forays when we just got here and Do you remember John Brown and the war between the states? And Mammy Ca'line would smile like at Aunt Margaret Brown and say 'I'm glad you survived it, sister, and I wonder what become of our Mama?' And they would just rock and rock."

Smoke was hanging over Buffalo like judgment. We rode silently through shortcuts we knew, and came at last into

my father's street. It was night. There were no children playing. In the middle of the block the door to my father's house
stood open and lighted as it had when my mother had died.
Fred parked the car and we unstuck ourselves from the seats,
tired and limp from laughing. My husband and my brother
took my hands and we walked slowly toward the light, toward
the family we had tried to escape.

We are orphans, my brother whispered. Very softly.

LUCY

I do not trouble my spirit to vindicate itself or be understood,
I see that the elementary laws never apologize.

—WALT WHITMAN, "Song of Myself"

I

"LUCILLE Sale, called Lucy, was the daughter of Caroline Donald and Sam Louis Sale," my Daddy would say. "They called him Uncle Louis like they did back then. This man, Bob Donald, bought Mammy Ca'line and set her to work in the orchard. They was big fruit growers and Ca'line worked in the orchards from when she was a little girl. One day when she had got big she was in the field and a carriage come by and stopped. And two old men was in it. It was Uncle Louis Sale and he was a slave but he was too old to work in the field and so his job was to drive his master in the carriage. His master was Old Man John F. Sale and he was a old man too, Lue, and blind. Uncle Louis had been given to his family as a boy. He was a present to their family. He was somebody and he was a present, a wedding present, Lue. And he was driving this carriage, an old man driving another old man, and he saw Ca'line in the orchard. And he stopped the horses and asked Old Man John F. to buy her for him for his wife. And Old Man John F. did. She was a young lady by then, Lue, and Uncle Louis had been born in 1777 but she was bought and went off to the Sale place and Old Man John F. married them legal cause he was a lawyer and they always said he was a good man. She lived there on the Sale place and they trained her to be a midwife and Mammy Ca'line and Uncle Louis had seven or more children, Lue, and one of the first ones was a girl. They called her Lucy but her name was Lucille. Like my own sister. And like you.

"Oh slavery, slavery," my Daddy would say. "It ain't something in a book, Lue. Even the good parts was awful."

2

MY FATHER looked like stone in a box. Like an old stone man caught in a box. He looks good, don't he, Lue? my sisters begged. Don't he look real good?

The room was heavy with flowers. My sisters had taken me to view the body and we were surrounded by cards bearing the names of my uncles and aunts and strange Polish names from our old neighborhood. I looked at the thin hook-nosed man in the box. He was still handsome, straight and military as he always was when he slept. He sleeps like he was dead, we used to laugh. His hand was curved as if his cane was in it, but his body was slightly on its side so that his missing leg was almost hidden. They were hiding his missing leg. The place where there was no leg was hidden. They were hiding his nothing. Nothing was hidden. They were missing nothing. I thought I was going to laugh. They were hiding where there was nothing to hide. Nothing was missing. I walked out of the room.

My father was an old man. My father had become an old man and I didn't even know it. This old man in a box was my father. Daddy had been an old man.

My sisters stood behind me. Don't he look good, Lue? They kept saying it. No, I finally answered. He's dead. I walked away.

*

My mother bore two children, a boy and a girl. My father was the father of four. He had three daughters by three different women, his first wife who died when she was twenty-one years old, my mother who triumphed with a son, and my youngest sister's mother who had been my father's lover when my mother was a bride. Our mothers had all known each other, had been friends. We were friends. My sisters and I. And my Mama had raised us all.

When Mama died they said he wouldn't last long. He'll have a hard time without Thel, they whispered, he can't make it without Thel. Even the widows and old girlfriends that gathered like birds nodded to each other. He needed Thel, he'll be gone soon.

But he fooled them. He was a strong man, a rock, and he lived on for ten years in his house, making a life. He took one of Mama's friends for his girlfriend, just as easily as he had married Mama when Edna Bell, his first wife and my sister Jo's mother, had died at twenty-one. And Mama's friend took care of him just as Mama had done, cooking and cleaning and being hollered at so much that once my children had asked me Is that lady Papa's maid or what? And I had answered No, not really, she's like my Mama was.

He lived on ten years in that house after Mama died, but my Mama lingered there too. His friend said she could hear her in the mornings early when it was time to get up and get his breakfast, and she would roll over and jump out of bed and run toward the kitchen, calling I'll get it, Thel, I'll get it. She was tough as a soldier, my father would say of my dead mother. She wasn't a Dahomey woman, but she was the Mama of one.

3

"WHEN you was born we was going to name you Georgia," Daddy told me once. "Because my mother's name was Georgia and your Mama's mother was named Georgia too. But when I saw you there you was so pretty I told your Mama I wanted to name you Thelma for her. And she said she didn't like her name and for me to give you another name with the Thelma. So I looked at you and you looked just like one of us and I thought about what Mammy Ca'line used to say about Dahomey women and I thought this child is one of us and I named you Lucille with the Thelma. Just like my sister Lucille and just like my real Grandmother Lucy. Genie, my Daddy's mother. First Black woman legally hanged in the state of Virginia."

He said Black like that, back then. And he would be looking proud.

Fred and I slept in the room that had once been mine. We were going to find a motel, but my sisters cried and asked us to stay with them. Just one night, you'll just be one night, they said. You ought to stay. And I looked at them and knew that they were right. I ought to stay. My sisters had stood by my father's bed while his leg had been amputated and Jo had cursed the nurses and made them clean his mess in the hospital and my sister Punkin had held his hand and they had bought him his wheelchair. And you ought to stay, they said to Sammy and me.

Sammy grumbled and took his suitcase to his old room and went out to visit with his own children and to get drunk, and Fred took our bags up to my old room. I looked at the women who were my sisters, one seven years older than I, the other six months younger, and thought about the other death we had shared in this house. Mama. My Mama. Jo's mother had died in another town when Jo was a baby, and Punkin's mother was alive and cooking quietly at last in her lover's kitchen. Three women who had loved Daddy. Three daughters who had loved Daddy. I shook my head and walked up the stairs to my old room. These are my sisters, I whispered to myself.

Lue, Jo cried up the steps to me. We're scared. He's gonna haunt us.

No he won't. I tried to comfort.

He sure will haunt me, Jo was crying. I'm bad and he'll haunt me for sure.

Not you, Lue, Punkin whispered. He won't bother you. You always was his heart.

4

"THEY named this daughter Lucille," my Daddy would say. "They say she was a tall skinny dark-skinned girl, look just like her mother. Mammy Ca'line. They say they couldn't get her to work as hard as the rest and she was quiet and thought she was better than the rest. Mammy Ca'line taught her that, they say, and I wouldn't be surprised if she did. They tell me she was mean. Lucy was mean always, I heard Aunt Margaret Brown say to Mammy Ca'line one time. And Mammy just said no she wasn't mean, she was strong. 'Strong women and weak men,' is what she said, 'sister, we be strong women and weak men.' And I run up to her and said Mammy, I ain't weak. And she just smiled at me and said 'Not you, mister, you won't be weak. You be a Sayle.'

"And Mammy was a midwife all through the war and her daughter Lucy worked with her sometime and after the war, after emancipation like they said, they just kept up delivering babies all around, white and Black. And the town just grew up, after the war, Lue, cause a lot of white folks come South to make money you know, off the South's trouble. And one of them was a carpetbagger from Connecticut. Named Harvey Nichols. The white man Lucy killed."

*

I waited all night for morning. Fred and I lay without sleeping in the room that had been my own and cried and talked about my Daddy. He had been a great storyteller. His life had been full of days and his days had been full of life.

5

MY FATHER was born in Bedford Virginia in 1902. His father Gene Sayle had died when he was a little boy and his mother had gone to work in the tobacco factory, leaving my father and his two brothers and one sister in the care of her dead husband's grandmother. My father's great-grandmother, who had been a slave. My father had left school in the second or third grade and could barely write more than his name, but he was an avid reader. He loved books. He had changed his name to Sayles (instead of Sayle) after finding a part of a textbook in which the plural was explained. There will be more than one of me, my father thought, and he added the *s* to his name. He had worked in coal mines and in laboring camps throughout the South, and had come North during a strike at a steel plant which hired him. He had married as a young man a girl named Edna Bell who died at twenty-one and he had then married her friend Thelma Moore, who died at forty-four. I won't get married again, he used to say, I'm a jinx, to young women.

He and Edna Bell had had a daughter Josephine, called Jo. He and Thelma Moore had had a daughter Thelma Lucille and then a neighbor woman had borne him a daughter Elaine, called Punkin, six months later. Two years after, he and Thelma became the parents of a son. A son. He had no other children and he never slept with his wife again. He said he had seen his son ever since he was a little boy in Virginia and he had never wanted any other thing.

And now he was dead. Fred and I lay and listened to the house. My Daddy and Mama were dead and their house was full of them.

6

"HARVEY Nichols was a white man," my Daddy would say, "who come South after the war to make money. He brought his wife and family down and bought himself a house and everything. And it was close to the Sale place and all the slaves had stayed there after emancipation because they said the Sales was good people, but they had just changed their last name to Sayle so people would know the difference. And this Harvey Nichols saw Lucy and wanted her and I say she must have wanted him too because like I told you, Lue, she was mean and didn't do nothing she didn't want to do and nobody could force her because she was Mammy Ca'line's child and everybody round there respected Mammy Ca'line so much. And her daughter Lucy had this baby boy by this Connecticut Yankee named Harvey Nichols. They named the baby Gene Sayle. He was my Daddy, Lue. Your own grandfather and Mammy Ca'line's grandson. But oh, Lue, he was born with a withered arm.

"Yes, Lord, he was born with a withered arm and when he was still just a baby Lucy waited by the crossroad one night for Harvey Nichols to come to her and when he rode up on a white horse, she cocked up a rifle she had stole and shot him off his horse and killed him, Lue. And she didn't run away, she didn't run away, she waited right there by the body with the rifle in her hand till the horse coming back empty-saddled to the stable brought a mob to see what had become of Harvey Nichols. And when they got to the crossroad they found Lucy standing there with the rifle in her hand. And they didn't lynch her, Lue, cause she was Mammy Ca'line's child, and from Dahomey women. That's what I believe. Mammy Ca'line got one of the lawyer Sale family to defend her daughter, cause they was all lawyers and preachers in that family. They had a legal trial and Lucy was found guilty. And hanged. Mammy Ca'line took the baby boy Genie and raised him and never let him forget who he was. I used to ask her sometime, Mammy, was you scared back then bout Granma Lucy? And she would look right at me and say 'I'm scared for you, mister, that's all.' She always called me mister. She said I was Mister Sayle. And Lue, I always was."

And Lucy was hanged. Was hanged, the lady whose name they gave me like a gift had her neck pulled up by a rope until the neck broke and I can see Mammy Ca'line standing straight as a soldier in green Virginia apart from the crowd of silent Black folk and white folk watching them and not the wooden frame swinging her child. And their shame making distance between them and her a real thing. And I know she made no sound but her mind closed round the picture like a frame and I know that her child made no sound and I turn in my chair and arch my back and make this sound for my two mothers and for all Dahomey women.

Later I would ask my father for proof. Where are the records, Daddy? I would ask. The time may not be right and it may just be a family legend or something. Somebody somewhere knows, he would say. And I would be dissatisfied and fuss with Fred about fact and proof and history until he told me one day not to worry, that even the lies are true. In history, even the lies are true.

And there would be days when we young Sayleses would be trying to dance and sing in the house and Sammy would miss a step and not be able to keep up to the music and he would look over in the corner of the room and holler "Damn Harvey Nichols." And we would laugh.

GENE

What is a man anyhow? what am I? what are you?

—WALT WHITMAN, "Song of Myself"

I

Daddy had surprised us and bought the house. Mama had thought he was throwing his money away, and would mumble about women being after him and him being bad after women, when one day he came home and threw a bankbook on the table, and some papers.

Every man has to do three things in life, he had said, plant a tree, own a house and have a son, and by God I've done two of them now. We had a house, he had bought a house and we were going to move. Punkin and Jo were married by then and I was soon going away to college. I was going to college. I had won a scholarship to Howard University and only Sammy would be at home. I was going away to college, a tall skinny kid who had never spent a night away from her Mama and now the daughters would all be gone and Daddy had bought a house.

He's getting old, Mama had whispered with great pride. She looked at him, glad that her time was coming. During the days that we were cleaning and packing and getting ready to move, Daddy would stop whatever he was doing and announce to us, I have had a son and now I own a house. All I got to do is plant a tree. And he would smile.

We children were not close to Daddy in those days. Punkin was walking the tight line stretched between her husband and her mother's children and us, her father's children, and she was quiet and withdrawn when we saw her. Jo had begun the slow dance between the streets and the cells that she practiced and practiced and Sammy had begun the young Black boy's initiation into wine and worse. And I had won a scholarship to Howard University. I was scared and proud and happy to get away. I had begun thinking of myself as special. Everybody said I was Daddy's favorite and I was the one who stayed with Mama and tried to watch out for her fits. I was a good girl. A smart girl. Lucille.

A week before we were to move I was to leave for Washington. The church gave a reception for me, the first person from our church to go to college, and everybody brought gifts and laughed and knew that I would make good. But I left Howard after two years. Lost my scholarship because I didn't study. I didn't have to, I thought. I didn't have to know about science and geography and things that I didn't want to know. I was a Dahomey woman. And so I came home to a disappointed and confused Mama and a Daddy who was furious and defensive and sad.

Feet of clay, he said to me. My idol got feet of clay. God sent you to college to show me that you got feet of clay.

Daddy, I argued with him, I don't need that stuff, I'm going to write poems. I can do what I want to do! I'm from Dahomey women!

You don't even know where that is, he frowned at me. You don't even know what it means.

And I ran to my room and cried all night and waited for the day. Because he was right. I cried and cried and listened.

Again. The house was full of noise. Sammy coming in and Jo crying and pacing the floor and Punkin going to the bathroom and being sick. But I didn't hear my father and I listened all night. He won't haunt you, Lue, they had said. He was always crazy about you.

2

"My Daddy died before I was six," my Daddy would say. "One day I was playing in the field and Aunt Margaret Brown hollered out the window Hush up that noise, your Daddy is dead. I hollered back I don't care. Because I wanted to play.

"My Daddy's name was Genie and he had a withered arm. He was born with it, oh but Lue, he was a handsome man. Always wore a derby and he was the color brown of cinnamon and he had real light brown eyes. Oh he had these light brown eyes from his Daddy being a white man and after his Mama Lucy was dead Mammy Ca'line took him and raised him. And she spoiled him too, spoiled him so bad till he was wild. And the women was crazy about him. He was crazy bout them too, he had a whole lot of women, Lue, when I go back home everybody my age looks just like me. And wild! On holidays the sheriff used to come to Mammy Ca'line and ask her to please keep Genie at home so the town could have the holiday, but she wouldn't do it. No sir. 'He can go where he please,' she would say, 'he from Dahomey women.' And when the holiday come he would put on his derby hat and go out in the field and pile up his withered arm with bricks and walk straight down the Main Street of town breaking out store windows. But they wouldn't lock him up. Sometime they would wait till his arm was empty of bricks and then they would drive him back home to Mammy Ca'line. And she would just shake her head at him."

Daddy, we would laugh, your Daddy was a crazy man. We had us a crazy grandfather. And my father would sigh "No he wasn't crazy. He was just somebody whose Mama and Daddy was dead."

And we would say Oh Daddy he was too crazy, you had a crazy man for a Daddy.

And my father would say "No, he didn't hardly get to be a man. He wasn't much past thirty years old when he died."

3

WHEN I was born my father was thirty-five years old. The handsomest man in town, Mama always said. She was twenty-one, a plump brown girl who had never had a real boyfriend. He was always a wonder to her, like someone from a foreign place, and she would watch him and listen to his words as if they were commandments. He had been called Mr. Sayles Lord when he was young and thought he was some kind of a God man. Once I asked him why he was so sure that he was going to heaven. God knows me, he said. God understands a man like me. Mama didn't really understand such a man. But she loved him. She cleaned his mess and fed him and took his abuse and called him "your crazy Daddy" in a voice thick with love until the day she dropped dead at forty-four years old. And he lived on for ten years after. And missed her every day.

He would say that he could hear her in the house. And sometimes when he was coming home from work, he said that he could see her get up from the chair by the window and walk to the front door to meet him. And he could hear somebody soft saying Samuel. She never called him anything but Samuel. Because that's his name, she would say.

4

"GENIE called me rock," my Daddy would say, "and he would take me into all them old beer gardens and sit me up on a corner of the bar. Then he'd walk round the bar hollering to all the other men that I could whip their boys and he'd take bets on it. Some of them would run and get their sons and he'd lift me up when they came back and he'd laugh 'Down and get on em, Rock!' and I would jump from his arms and whip that other boy. Oh my Mama would be mad at him about that but she didn't never say anything to him about it. Her name was Georgia Hatcher and her family had belonged to the Lees. Genie was a barber at that time and he would go round to people's houses and cut their hair. First thing I ever remember is the sound of him coming home from cutting hair and singing at the top of his voice. Just singing as loud as he could. And my Mama would be just grinning cause he was so handsome and so wild. She didn't know I could see her but I remember her watching out for him and grinning, and Mammy Ca'line watching too and shaking her head and whispering Genie Genie Genie. We always been strong women and weak men, Lue, up till me.

"When my Daddy died I said I didn't care cause I wanted to play. And my Mama went to work in the tobacco plant and left us with Mammy Ca'line. After a little while my Mama married again. A man named Luke Stevens and, Lue, she had two more sons and a daughter. Mr. Luke was a good man, a real good man, but Mammy Ca'line spoiled us so, you know, and we treated him bad, we Sayles. She told us we didn't have to do what he said, you know. She shouldn't have told us that cause he was always good to us and he treated my Mama real good. But Mammy Ca'line would tell us that we was Sayle people and we didn't have to obey nobody. You a Sayle, she would say. You from Dahomey women.

"Only time I ever saw my Mama cry was she was sitting at the table reading a letter. It was night and the tobacco plant was laying off and so she was doing some day work and coming home to help Mammy Ca'line clean up after us at night. Some of her friends had gone off to New York City to look for work and they had wrote her a letter telling her to come too. But she had us kids, you know, and couldn't go. I asked her how come she wanted to go to New York City and she started crying and said 'I just want to see some things. I want to walk in the North and see some things.' Not long after that is when she married Mr. Luke. I asked Mammy Ca'line about why did my Mama want to see the North and everything. And she just looked at me. Then I asked her did she ever want to see some other place beside Virginia, and 'I already seen it, mister' is what she said."

5

AFTER my mother was thirty-five years old she began having seizures. Epilepsy. Daddy was furious with her for having fits. For something happening that he couldn't understand and couldn't help. He would shout at her to stop sitting in that chair by the window, her chair. That chair is giving you fits, he would say. She went to clinics and took tests but she had the seizures regularly until she died. And after she was dead, my father began having them. Mild ones, not like my mother's, terrible to look at, but seizures all the same.

He had worked in a steel mill for over thirty years and had contracted emphysema. Emphysema and fits. And a brain tumor. He discovered he had a brain tumor during the course of a hospital stay because of the emphysema and the doctors wanted to operate. At first he refused. Nobody cuts my family, he insisted. But my sisters and my brother and I fussed and fussed until he finally agreed to it. They removed a tumor about the size of an orange from his brain and he was up and out of the hospital in a matter of weeks. And just the same. We saw no difference in him.

Later his leg died. Just shriveled up and turned black and died and the doctors said that they had to amputate it or the death would spread throughout his body. And so he let them cut it off and he got a cane. He would smile and point to the empty place. Yeah, they got my leg but they didn't get me, he would boast.

SAMUEL

All goes onward and outward, nothing collapses,
And to die is different from what any one supposed, and
   luckier.

—WALT WHITMAN, "Song of Myself"

I

THE MORNING of my father's funeral was grey and wet. Everything cried. Jo and Punkin and I stood waiting to be driven to the church in our stiff new black hats and veils. Sammy stood unsteady in the things that Fred had rushed out in the early morning rain and bought him. We were silent, a quiet place in the middle of girlfriends and cousins and my Aunt Lucille who had come from New Jersey in the night. She was standing as she always stood, stiff and military in the rain, surrounded by people who didn't like her. Daddy had loved his sister dearly and we resented his affection. She don't never call him, we would whisper, he always got to call her and she always want him to send for her. She don't even think about him and he crazy bout her.

She and I were in the first car and she turned to me when it came and took my arm. Lucille and Lucille. She was an old woman, an old soldier. I took her hand as we stepped into the car. I too was straight and quiet. Mammy Ca'line's great-granddaughter and great-great-granddaughter. Dahomey women. We rode to the church in silence.

2

"THE GENERATIONS of Caroline Donald, born free among the Dahomey people in 1822 and died free in Bedford Virginia in 1910," my Daddy would say, "and Sam Louis Sale, born a slave in America in 1777 and died a slave in the same place in around 1860
are Dabney and Gabriel and Sam and Helen and John and Lucille,
called Lucy
who had a son named Gene by a man named Harvey Nichols and then
she killed him,
and this boy Gene with a withered arm had three sons and a daughter
named Willie and Harvey and Samuel and Lucille
and Samuel who is me
named his boy Sam and
his daughter Lucille.
We fooled em, Lue, slavery was terrible but we fooled them old people. We come out of it better than they did."

3

MY FATHER was laid in the ground between his wives. The stones seemed strange to me. Edna Sayles. Thelma Sayles. I had never thought of Jo's mother as a Sayles before and the name seemed too big in my mouth. Punkin's mother waited, cooking at the house, and I thought of her and wondered where she would lie. My father was lowered into the ground between his wives and my face was wet before I realized it. I wanted to tell him something, my insides screamed. I remember everything. I believe. Everything shook and my Aunt Lucille was shaking my arm and crying. Crying without shame quietly and straight as a soldier. Mammy Mammy she was whispering in her tears, Mammy it's 1969, and we're still here. I held her hand tightly. Lucille and Lucille.

My father bumped against the earth. Like a rock.

THELMA

They are alive and well somewhere,
The smallest sprout shows there is really no death,
And if ever there was, it led forward life, and does not wait
    at the end to arrest it,
And ceas'd the moment life appear'd.

—WALT WHITMAN, "Song of Myself"

I

WELL

my Mama was from Georgia. My Mama was born in Rome Georgia in 1914. She used to tell us that she was from Rome, and when we were little we thought she was Italian. But she was a round brown lady from Georgia, and as Daddy said, "Everybody from Georgia glad to be *from* there." Her father has sent for her and her mother and sisters and brothers to come to Depew after he had been North awhile. He had come on the same train as my Daddy, in the strikebreaking. My Daddy and my grandfather were friends and my Mama was twelve years younger than my Daddy. My Daddy's first wife was a good friend of my Mama and so was my little sister's mother and so was his last girlfriend. All friends.

When the colored people came to Depew they came to be a family. Everybody began to be related in thin ways that last and last. The generations of white folks are just people but the generations of colored folks are families.

Depew is where I was born. Depew New York, in 1936. Roosevelt time. It was a small town, mostly Polish, all its life turned like a machine around the steel mill. We lived in a house on Muskingum Street, and my Mama's family lived on Laverack. My grandparents lived in this big frame house on Laverack Street with one toilet. And in that house were my Mama's family, the Moores, and a lot of other people, lines of people, old and young.

There was an old man who was a deacon, a pillar of the church. I remember once in prayer meeting, he was praying and the lights went out...a blackout, you know, in the second world war. And he was deep in the middle of his best praying. He was a very religious man, a deacon, and all of a sudden the lights went out and he looked up and shouted "Dammit, now, God!" then went on with his prayer. A good prayer too.

Our whole family lived there. In Depew. All the Moores, I mean. All around the steel mill. My grandfather and Daddy and uncles and all our men. Turning around the plant.

Depew. One of the earliest things I remember was the goat in the backyard. Our house was on top of a big hill and across the yard and down the hill in the back were the Moores. And Grandma kept a goat back there. Depew.

The closest big city was Buffalo, twelve miles away. One time Daddy walked there to buy a dining room set. He was the first colored man in Depew to have a dining room set. And he walked to Buffalo to get it. He got it on credit from Peoples', a store where they gave colored people credit back then. This is what it was like: you got this credit from Peoples' store and the Peoples' man would come around to your house every week and collect. It would just be fifty cents or a dollar, but that was some money in those times and you know it went on for so long. So long. My Daddy paid something to the Peoples' man for as long as I can remember. Me and my brother used to hate him because he would come over every Saturday and collect and Daddy called him Mr. Pitterman but he called Daddy Sam. And his name was Samuel too, Samuel Pitterman, and if Daddy could be called Sam so could he. But he never was. Every Saturday he would come over and even after we moved to Buffalo when I was five or six, he would collect and then he would sit with Daddy on the porch and they would talk over old days. And Daddy would look forward to it.

He used to carry merchandise in the trunk of his car, Sam Pitterman, and he would sell things out of it. One Christmas he gave me and Punkin matching white crepe skirts, pleated all around. We put them in the bottom drawer of our dresser where the mice had gnawed and left them there.

Anyway, my Daddy wanted to have this dining room set and he walked to Buffalo to get it and when he got to Peoples' the salesman there told him he didn't need a dining room set. And Daddy told the man that his great-grandmother was a Dahomey woman and he could have anything he wanted. And so he got it. And walked back home, and they delivered the set. First colored man to own a dining room set in Depew New York.

Roosevelt time. War time.

I remember when my uncle came home from the second world war, my Mama's baby brother. He belonged to the ninety-second division, which was the colored infantry, I think, and they had been in Italy. Oh we were all so proud of him, and one afternoon my Grandma was sitting by the window looking out, and my aunt came into the kitchen from getting the mail and said "Mother, we got a letter from

Buddy…and Here It Is!" And my uncle come grinning through the door with his soldier's suit on and oh my Grandma Moore laughed and cried and laughed again. I always remember how my Grandma Moore just sang out "Oh here's my Buddy Buddy Buddy Buddy!"

She was my grandmother that called me Genius. My Mama's mother. The Moores moved to Buffalo a while after we did, and they moved to downtown. She believed that I was twelve years old until the day she died, and I was married and pregnant. Always thought I was twelve, and she called me Genius because she knew I went to college.

When I went away to college, well, that was some time. People couldn't get it straight that I was going to Howard and not Harvard. Nobody in our family had graduated from high school at that time, and at that time no member of our church had ever gone to college. I had won this scholarship, you know, and they gave me this big party at the church. The Baptist church.

Now we didn't know a thing about going to college. I remember I took my Grandma's wedding trunk, all held together with rope. Me and Mama went over to Peoples' and bought me a black silk skirt and a red see-through blouse and we packed Grandma Moore's wedding trunk. When they delivered it at Howard, all those ritzy girls from Chicago and Texas, oh I was so embarrassed I went down at night to pick it up. This old trunk with thick rope around it and Georgia Moore written in ink. Anyway, I went away to college, and before I left I had to go and say goodby to everybody.

And we went to see Grandma and she was watching for us, and when we started down her block, she ran out on the porch hollering "Everybody, Everybody, Here come my Genius!" And all her neighbor people come running out on the porch. And here I come, here I come.

My Grandma Moore told me to behave myself away from home, and I promised that I would. I had never been away from home and my own people before and let me tell you I was scared but I didn't let on. Then she asked me "Where was Moses when the lights went out?" and I said "Grandma, I just don't know," and she said "Well, that's all right, just keep your dress tail down," and I said "Yes, ma'am," because I understood that part.

There was another old lady, older than Grandma, named Miss Washington, and she had been born in slavery. I went to see her and she gave me these doilies, all these doilies she had crocheted with her own hands. She told me about when she was a tiny girl and Mr. Lincoln had come by in a parade and her mother had picked her up and made her wave her hand. She told me about this proud thing and gave me these doilies to take to college, and I went off to school.

I was sixteen years old and went away to college and I had never slept a night away from my Mama and when me and my friend Retha and my friend Betty got to Washington they had this huge train station. I had never seen a place like that and I started to almost cry and I said to Retha that as soon as I ate I was going back home. Then a Howard man came up to us and looked at Betty all little and cute with her college clothes and her name tag on and said "You'll love it here, and we'll love you," and he turned to me and asked me if I was her mother. From that moment I knew I wouldn't last. And I didn't. Two years. That was all.

But what a two years it was! What a time! I was from New York, so that was a big deal, and I was a drama major, so that was a big deal too. At that time, at Howard, if you weren't light-skinned or had long hair you had to have something pretty strong going for you. Well, I was a drama major from New York. They didn't know that Buffalo is a long way from New York City, and for them that did know, I could lay claim to Canada, so it worked out well enough.

My Daddy wrote me a letter my first week there, and my Daddy could only write his name. But he got this letter together and it said "Dear Lucilleman, I miss you so much but you are there getting what we want you to have be a good girl signed your daddy." I cried and cried because it was the greatest letter I ever read or read about in my whole life. Mama wrote me too and her letter said, "Your daddy has written you a letter and he worked all day."

Being away from home, I didn't even know how to do it. I used to think I was going to starve to death. Nobody had any notion of what I needed or anything. One time Mama sent me a box full of tuna fish. I hid it under my bed and at night I would take it out and open can after can of tuna fish. And I was always afraid I'd make a mistake and Daddy would find out. I knew he'd know whatever I did. Whatever I did. But I was proud. The first Thanksgiving I went back home and now I had only been gone since September but when I stepped off the train Daddy and my sister Jo were there and Jo said "Oh, she don't look so different," but I started talking with a Washington accent and I even had to try to remember the way home. I was a mess. I thought everything seemed so little.

When we moved to Buffalo, we were moving to the big city. I was six or seven, maybe even five, and we moved to Buffalo one night in a truck. We thought it was the biggest place in the world. The lady who owned the house had left a doll for me in the attic, and that doll and that attic and that whole house smelled like new days. Purdy Street.

My Daddy was from Bedford Virginia and he left home when he was a boy and did a lot of moving around. He was so handsome they called him Mr. Sayles Lord, and when he'd walk down the street women would come out of their houses and say it. He used to go to dances and sometimes in the middle of a dance he would get tired and throw his hat down and shout The Dance Is Over, and all the people would stop playing music and dancing and go home.

He came to Depew when a train came through the South offering colored men jobs and a trip North. And he got on in Virginia and my Grandpa Moore had got on in Georgia. When my Daddy got North he worked in the plant and he married Edna Bell, my sister Jo's mother, who died when she was only twenty-one years old. He used to say that they didn't know why she died until one night she came to him in a dream and told him to have them check her for consumption because that's what she had. Any they checked and found it. Tuberculosis. Consumption.

TB. You know just a few of us in our family have never had TB. I never had it. Some people had it twice. I never had it, and my cousins used to say it was because I was a good girl.

When I was a girl if my cousins would curse around me they would always say "Excuse me, Lucille." They would never say anything about anything around me and that's why there were all patches of things I learned late. I had a girlfriend who used to talk to me about dope though. Before I went away to school she was walking the street, and she took me up to where she stayed with this man who was a pimp, and they had a list of places in Washington D.C. where they said they better not hear about me going. They didn't want me to disgrace them in Washington D.C. I paid attention, too, because I always wanted to do the right thing. I always wanted to.

I have two sisters, half-sisters, and a brother. I used to be a little bit scared of my older sister Jo. She's getting older now, though, and she's playing mother to her kids and grandmother to their kids in a big way. Last time I saw her she was standing on Daddy's porch with her arm around her boyfriend Bobby and he was waving. Bobby, her boyfriend, only had one eye. She had another boyfriend with one eye once and I heard Daddy say to himself one time "All her men just got one eye, can't she get a man got two good eyes?"

There were a lot of small-time folks like that in Buffalo. Lot of very nice people who were also small-time crooks mostly

because there wasn't much else to be. Just about everybody was on the welfare, giving up a little bit of everything to get on the city. A little bit of everything and a whole lot of pride. There was an older colored lady that was a caseworker and everybody hated to see her coming she was so mean. Mama and Daddy never were on the welfare and it made us proud. They made us proud, wanted us to be.

A lady down the street from us had a civil service job, just nothing, just a file clerk or like that, but Daddy used to tell me when she would pass by "Lue, you keep being a good girl and keep your grades good and you can be just like her." She married a man who was a chiropractor and published a little newspaper. He also had a shoe repair shop and he used to fix the shoes himself. He would be in there late at night tacking shoes together with a tack hammer. His shop was across the street from where we lived, next-door to the grocery shop owned by two white women from Canada. They used to sue Mama all the time because she would get credit and get credit without telling Daddy and not pay it back and finally they would sue her. They would send summonses to the house. They used to always tell me to get away, get away, and want to take me to Canada for a while. They thought I seemed like a nervous child.

I seemed a lot of things. I used to go to the black-market meat store during the war and it was always packed and I would lean on the counter and it seemed like I was going to faint and they would always wait on me before it was really my turn. I seemed a lot of things.

One time Mama bought herself a wedding ring set and of course she couldn't pay for it. She must have known that.

But she had said to me once that I should always try to have something I could pawn, and anyway she had never had a wedding ring, so she bought these rings. When they were going to sue her she sent me, a small child too, downtown to take them back and to tell the jeweler that I was the lady next-door's little girl and Mrs. Sayles said she was returning the rings. He must have seen through that, but he didn't let on.

Oh she made magic, she was a magic woman, my Mama. She was not wise in the world but she had magic wisdom. She was twenty-one years old when she got married but she had had to stay home and help take care of her brothers and sisters. And she had married Daddy right out of her mother's house. Just stayed home, then married Daddy who had been her friend Edna Bell's husband after Edna Bell died. She never went out much. She used to sit and hum in this chair by the window. After my brother was born, she never slept with my Daddy again. She never slept with anybody, for twenty years. She used to tell me "Get away, get away. I have not had a normal life. I want you to have a natural life. I want you to get away."

A lot of people were always telling me to get away.

She used to sit in this chair by the window and hum and rock. Some Sundays in the summertime me and her used to go for walks over to the white folks section to look in their windows and I would tell her when I grew up I was going to take her to a new place and buy her all those things.

Once in a while we would go to the movies, me and her. But after she started having her fits I would worry her so much with Are you all right Ma and How do you feel Ma that we didn't go as often. Once I asked her if she was all right and she said she would be fine if I would leave her alone.

Mostly on Friday nights when Daddy had gone out and the other kids had gone out too we would get hamburgers and pop from the store and sit together and after we got TV we would watch TV. On New Year's Eve we would wait up until midnight and I would play Auld Lang Syne on the piano while me and my Mama sang and then we would go to bed.

Oh she was magic. If there were locks that were locked tight, she could get a little thing and open them. She could take old bent hangers and rags and make curtains and hang drapes. She ironed on chairs and made cakes every week and everybody loved her. Everybody.

When Daddy bought the house away from Purdy Street, Mama didn't know that he had been saving his money. One day he just took us to see this house he was buying. I was going away to college that fall and Punkin was off and married and we were scattering but he had bought us this house to be together in. Because we were his family and he loved us and wanted us to be together. He was a strong man, a strong family man, my Daddy. So many people knew him for a man in a time when it wasn't so common. And he lived with us, our Daddy lived in our house with us, and that wasn't common then either. He was not a common man. Now, he did some things, he did some things, but he always loved his family.

He hurt us all a lot and we hurt him a lot, the way people who love each other do, you know. I probably am better off than any of us, better off in my mind, you know, and I credit Fred for that. Punkin she has a hard time living in the world and so does my brother and Jo has a hard time and gives one too. And a lot of all that is his fault, has something to do with him.

And Mama, Mama's life was—seemed like—the biggest waste in the world to me, but now I don't know, I'm not sure any more. She married him when she was a young twenty-one and he was the only man she ever knew and he was the only man she ever loved and how she loved him! She adored him. He'd stay out all night and in the morning when he came home he'd be swinging down the street and she would look out the window and she'd say loud "Here come your crazy Daddy." And the relief and joy would make her face shine. She used to get up at five every morning to fix his breakfast for him and she one time fell down the back steps and broke her ankle and didn't see about it until after she had fixed breakfast, had gotten back up the steps and finished.

She would leave him. She would leave him and come in every morning at five o'clock to fix his breakfast because "your Daddy works hard," she would fuss, "you know you can't fix him a decent meal."

She would sit in the movies. She would leave him and sit in the movies and I would see her there and try to talk and make things right. I always felt that I was supposed to make things right, only I didn't know how, I didn't know how. I used to laugh and laugh at the dinner table till they thought I was crazy but I was so anxious to make things right.

I never knew what to do. One time they were arguing about something and he was going to hit her and my sister Punkin, who had a different mother, she ran and got the broom and kept shouting "If you hit Mama I'll kill you" at Daddy. My brother and I didn't do anything but stand there and it was our Mama but we didn't do anything because we didn't know what to do.

Another time they were arguing and I was in the kitchen washing dishes and all of a sudden I heard my Mama start screaming and fall down on the floor and I ran into the room and she was rolling on the floor and Daddy hadn't touched her, she had just started screaming and rolling on the floor. "What have you done to her," I hollered. Then "What should I do, what should I do?" And Daddy said "I don't know, I don't know, I don't know, she's crazy," and went out. When he left, Mama lay still, and then sat up and leaned on me and whispered "Lue, I'm just tired, I'm just tired."

The last time ever I saw her alive she had been undergoing tests to find out what caused her epilepsy and I leaned over to kiss her and she looked at me and said "The doctors took a test and they say I'm not crazy. Tell your Daddy."

I wanted to make things better. I used to lay in bed at night and listen for her fits. And earlier than that, when I was younger, a little girl, I would lay awake and listen for their fights. One night they were shouting at each other and my sister Punkin whispered out of her stillness "Lue, are you awake?" "No," I mumbled. She stirred a little. "That's good," she said.

*

I wanted to make things right. I always thought I was supposed to. As if there was a right. As if I knew what right was.
As if I knew.

My Mama dropped dead in a hospital hall one month
before my first child was born. She had gone to take a series
of tests to try to find out the cause of her epilepsy. I went to
visit her every day and we laughed and talked about the baby
coming. Her first grandchild. On this day, Friday, February
13, it was raining but I started out early because I had not
gone to see her the day before. My aunt and my Uncle Buddy
were standing in the reception area and as I came in they
rushed to me saying "Wait, Lue, wait, it's not visiting hours
yet." After a few minutes I noticed other people going on
toward the wards and I started up when my aunt said "Where
you going, Lue?" and I said "Up to see my Mama," and they
said all together "Lue Lue your Mama's dead." I stopped. I
said "That's not funny." Nobody laughed, just looked at me,
and I fell, big as a house with my baby, back into the telephone
booth, crying "Oh Buddy Oh Buddy, Buddy, Buddy."

One month and ten days later another Dahomey woman
was born, but this one was mixed with magic.

Things don't fall apart. Things hold. Lines connect in thin
ways that last and last and lives become generations made
out of pictures and words just kept. "We come out of it better than they did, Lue," my Daddy said, and I watch my six
children and know we did. They walk with confidence through
the world, free sons and daughters of free folk, for my Mama
told me that slavery was a temporary thing, mostly we was

free and she was right. And she smiled when she said it and
Daddy smiled too and saw that my sons are as strong as my
daughters and it had been made right.

And I could tell you about things we been through, some
awful ones, some wonderful, but I know that the things that
make us are more than that, our lives are more than the days
in them, our lives are our line and we go on. I type that and
I swear I can see Ca'line standing in the green of Virginia,
in the green of Afrika, and I swear she makes no sound but
she nods her head and smiles.

The generations of Caroline Donald born in Afrika in 1823
and Sam Louis Sale born in America in 1777 are
Lucille
who had a son named
Genie
who had a son named
Samuel
who married
Thelma Moore and the blood became Magic and their
daughter is
Thelma Lucille
who married Fred Clifton and the blood became whole and
their children are
Sidney
Fredrica
Gillian
Alexia   four daughters and
Channing
Graham   two sons,
and the line goes on.
"Don't you worry, mister, don't you worry."

Backward I see in my own days where I sweated through fog
   with linguists and contenders,
I have no mockings or arguments, I witness and wait.

—Walt Whitman, "Song of Myself"

OTHER NEW YORK REVIEW CLASSICS

For a complete list of titles, visit www.nyrb.com.

SIGIZMUND KRZHIZHANOVSKY The Letter Killers Club
SIGIZMUND KRZHIZHANOVSKY Memories of the Future
SIGIZMUND KRZHIZHANOVSKY The Return of Munchausen
SIGIZMUND KRZHIZHANOVSKY Unwitting Street
K'UNG SHANG-JEN The Peach Blossom Fan
GIUSEPPE TOMASI DI LAMPEDUSA The Professor and the Siren
D.H. LAWRENCE The Bad Side of Books: Selected Essays
GERT LEDIG The Stalin Front
MARGARET LEECH Reveille in Washington: 1860–1865
PATRICK LEIGH FERMOR Between the Woods and the Water
PATRICK LEIGH FERMOR The Broken Road
PATRICK LEIGH FERMOR Mani: Travels in the Southern Peloponnese
PATRICK LEIGH FERMOR Roumeli: Travels in Northern Greece
PATRICK LEIGH FERMOR A Time of Gifts
PATRICK LEIGH FERMOR A Time to Keep Silence
PATRICK LEIGH FERMOR The Traveller's Tree
PATRICK LEIGH FERMOR The Violins of Saint-Jacques
NIKOLAI LESKOV Lady Macbeth of Mtsensk: Selected Stories of Nikolai Leskov
D.B. WYNDHAM LEWIS AND CHARLES LEE (EDITORS) The Stuffed Owl
SIMON LEYS The Death of Napoleon
SIMON LEYS The Hall of Uselessness: Collected Essays
MARGARITA LIBERAKI Three Summers
GEORG CHRISTOPH LICHTENBERG The Waste Books
JAKOV LIND Soul of Wood and Other Stories
H.P. LOVECRAFT AND OTHERS Shadows of Carcosa: Tales of Cosmic Horror
DWIGHT MACDONALD Masscult and Midcult: Essays Against the American Grain
CURZIO MALAPARTE Diary of a Foreigner in Paris
CURZIO MALAPARTE Kaputt
CURZIO MALAPARTE The Kremlin Ball
CURZIO MALAPARTE The Skin
JANET MALCOLM In the Freud Archives
JEAN-PATRICK MANCHETTE Fatale
JEAN-PATRICK MANCHETTE Ivory Pearl
JEAN-PATRICK MANCHETTE The Mad and the Bad
JEAN-PATRICK MANCHETTE Nada
JEAN-PATRICK MANCHETTE The N'Gustro Affair
JEAN-PATRICK MANCHETTE No Room at the Morgue
OSIP MANDELSTAM The Selected Poems of Osip Mandelstam
THOMAS MANN Reflections of a Nonpolitical Man
OLIVIA MANNING Fortunes of War: The Balkan Trilogy
OLIVIA MANNING Fortunes of War: The Levant Trilogy
OLIVIA MANNING School for Love
JAMES VANCE MARSHALL Walkabout
GUY DE MAUPASSANT Afloat
GUY DE MAUPASSANT Alien Hearts
GUY DE MAUPASSANT Like Death
JAMES McCOURT Mawrdew Czgowchwz
WILLIAM McPHERSON Testing the Current
DAVID MENDEL Proper Doctoring: A Book for Patients and their Doctors
W.S. MERWIN (TRANSLATOR) The Life of Lazarillo de Tormes
MEZZ MEZZROW AND BERNARD WOLFE Really the Blues
HENRI MICHAUX Miserable Miracle
JESSICA MITFORD Hons and Rebels